# People Live Here

George Wong

**This is a desert.**

3

# People live here.

This is a plain.

# People live here.

This is a mountain.

# People live here.

This is a forest.

15

**People live here.**

This is a wetland.

**People live here.**

This is a river.

# People live here.